I0116846

# Values and Unintended Consequences:
## *A Workbook*

*Kathryn Alexander, MA*

**Resilient Planet Publishing**
Spokane, Washington

© 2006-2013, Kathryn Alexander All
rights reserved.

No part of this book may be reproduced
in any manner without written
permission from the publisher, except
in the case of quotes used in critical
articles and reviews.

RESILIENT PLANET PRESS 9116 E
Sprague #585 Spokane, WA 99206
http://www.kathrynalexanderlive.com

ISBN-10: 0692261265
ISBN-13: 978-0692261262

## ACKNOWLEDGEMENTS

There are SO many who have contributed to this work! Ludwig von Bertalanffy – my first exposure to systems thinking and Béla H. Bánáthy and Peter Senge who deepened it, and Jane Jacobs who open my eyes to values as systems. Thank you!

# Table of Contents

# Values and Unintended Consequences

## *Introduction*

This small workbook is designed for you to use to begin to better understand your own values system and that of your family. Values are an inherent part of us and for some are what defines them as individuals. Each person acts from their cherished values, especially when under pressure, and sometimes that can cause unintended consequences. These consequences can be as small as a surprise reaction or as large as a more devastating catastrophe.

This workbook is designed to help you think in new ways about your values and those of your family. At the end you will find a series of work pages where you can begin to clarify your thinking about your own value system and that of your family.

## *Definition*

All values fall into one or two broad categories: moral values and non-moral values. In this chapter, the terms "moral" and "non-moral" are used without any religious connotations.

Moral values have to do with right and wrong, good and evil. They guide your behavior with the force of obligation. They form the basis for judgments of moral responsibility and guide such ethical behavior as telling the truth, keeping agreements, and not injuring others. Associated with moral values are such character traits as honesty, loyalty, and fairness. Moral statements often contain words such as "must...ought...should... never...always".

Non-moral values have to do with tastes, preferences, and styles. They relate to what is desirable and undesirable, as opposed to what is right and wrong or good and evil. Non-moral values carry no sense of obligation. There is no moral responsibility connected with accepting or rejection a non-moral value.

The traits associated with non-moral values tend to be personality traits like charm, shyness, or cheerfulness, as opposed to character traits like honesty or fairness. The activities that come out of non-moral values are merely preferred, not dictated: going to the ballgame instead of to a movie, reading a book instead of watching television. Non-moral values are a lot more plentiful than moral values, since they are expressions of your attitudes toward all sorts of objects, concepts, and experiences: cars, paintings, art, knowledge, pleasure, democracy, history, sports, hobbies, etc.

Statements of non-moral value often contain the same words as statements of moral value, but examination shows that the words as statements of moral value, are not meant in an absolute, normative sense.

In this workbook we will be talking about **very specific** values that are held in a "moral" sense. If this subject interests you please see our work on *Values Clarification*.

## Values as Systems

One thing that is unique to the Kathryn Alexander approach to values, is our understanding of them as systems. Before we get into how we see them as systems, let's expand on what we mean by "systems" and then we'll look at the implications that has as we apply our values to real life situations.

### *Systems Theory*

All living systems share certain characteristics:
- All living systems have a purpose; and they are wholes that can be taken apart.

- Living systems consist of parts and processes and all of the parts consist of interrelated parts/processes.

- All of the parts are interdependent, but each part has an affect on the whole, but not all the time and not independently.

- Systems effects are non-linear – results or consequences happen at different time times and places than expected.

- All living systems are nested.

What does all this mean?

## Living Systems Have Purpose

We are only taking about living systems and NOT mechanical systems. So these characteristics apply to biological and social systems, i.e. all human systems.

One of the things that makes humans so complex is that we have a number of purposes. Most biological systems (ecologies) have simple purposes; stay alive and reproduce. Humans complicate things. We have those purposes, but we also want to succeed (how ever we define that) and we may also want to exact vengeance and have other emotional needs met, so they become "purposes".

The key here is that a "purpose" however it is defined *at that moment* will dictate how people behave. The "purpose" describes *why* the behavior took place.

### Living Systems Are Wholes
You are the living system you are most familiar with. You, as a person, are a whole. You *can* be taken apart (medicine is getting very good at this), but doing so affects the entire rest of the system (your body). For example, if you break your little toe your whole body begins to compensate. That's a small example of interrelatedness. If you are taken apart, that part (your hand, for instance) has no function. It functions *only* as part of the whole. In families this is particularly important because we tend to think that each person is important when, in reality, it's the *interaction* between family members that makes the family work.

### Non-Linearity
Most of us think of cause and effect as sort of a "push-pull" affair. You push there and it moves here. There is a direct "line" between the cause and the effect. In living systems that is not the case. My best example is a story.

At the Ritz Carlton hotel they had been making lots of changes and were very proud of their results. So proud that they decided to offer $100 to any guest who order from room service who was unhappy. Suddenly they discovered that they were paying out way too many of these $100 "gifts". People were up set because their food was cold upon arrival.

Now think a moment – what would you do about this situation? Castigate the delivery folks? Hire new ones?

Ritz Carlton asked the delivery folks what was happening. They were told that the delivery folks had to wait for the elevators, and that's why the dinners were cold.

Now think a moment – what would you do about this situation? Set aside one elevator for deliveries? Put in a new elevator? Give the delivery folks hot boxes to protect the food?

So they researched the next step to find out why the delivery folks had to wait. The reason they discovered was that the maids were using the elevators.

Now what's your solution? Hire more maids? Dedicate an elevator? Make them take the stairs?

The next research was to discover why the maids were going up and down. The reason was that there were not enough towels.

So, the food was being delivered cold because there were not enough towels.

This is what is meant by non-linear. There is NO direct line between the presenting problem and the solution. By asking "Why" five times you can get to the root cause. This is also why it is so hard to really solve problems in families. The solutions are NOT readily apparent.

The same is true of values issues. Good values can cause bad problems and good values *misapplied* can cause corruption.

### Feedback Loops
Feedback is crucial for systems. Feedback is the process of getting information into the system to keep it fulfilling its purpose. Without feedback the system would become chaotic and out of control. Feedback allows the system to self-correct.

Feedback comes in two flavors:

| + | − |
|---|---|
| Accelerating Reinforcing | Dampening Balancing |

Neither is good or bad, both can be good and both can require drastic change to maintain the direction toward purpose.

Feedback that is accelerating could be information about how your work is received. If your spouse yells at you because you did something the wrong way, if your siblings tease you for an outburst, if no one pays attention to you, then you are in an accelerating/reinforcing loop of feedback that appears to tell you, you are not valued.

On-the-other-hand, if your spouse tells you in front of others how good your work was, if your siblings ask to see what you did, or if your siblings ask you what you did so they can improve what they do, then you are in an accelerating/reinforcing loop that tells you, you have value.

If your spouse commends you in front of others, others ask to see it, and one of them points out areas of weakness, then you have just experienced a balancing/dampening loop that counters the accelerating/reinforcing loop and BOTH suggest that you have value.

Both accelerating/reinforcing and dampening/balancing loops are important and necessary. It is the interaction that keeps a system (in the above example – you) on its correct course. Feedback is crucial – seek it!

# The Kathryn Alexander Approach to Values

## *The Value Systems*

For our purposes we look at two distinct systems. The first is the Protective system. Its purpose is protection. There are about 15 separate values that compose this system. The second system is the Effective system and its purpose is effectiveness. It too is composed of about 15 separate values. Then there is a third system of shared values that both systems endorse.

We look at very specific values. Some of them are not values that would naturally come to your mind. Their use is so automatic that they are invisible. As they are listed and described, look into your own behavior and see if they show up.

## *Protective Values*

The Protective system is very old. It formed when positions in the community were very fixed and often hereditary. These values originally applied to the military, government and religious sectors. Now we all have them.

## Be Loyal

Loyalty is often seen as undying and unequivocal support. The underlying belief is that a person should be so trusted that there are no questions allowed about the leaders actions. There is no public dissent allowed and there is no hesitation in following the leaders orders.

## Take Vengeance

When some one is disloyal then they should be made to pay for their transgression. People who do not follow the party line should be punished or penalized in some way for their behavior.

## Deceive for the Sake of the Task

Lying and subterfuge are permissible if they will help get the job done. Decoys, deception, and other methods of hiding what is being done are OK if the end is honorable. Think military, law enforcement and that little white lie that eases an uncomfortable situation.

## Obedience and Discipline are Expected

People who are very disciplined and obedient are prized and held up for admiration. Independent behavior is not tolerated and can even be suspect.

## Exclusivity is the Norm

It takes effort and perhaps some kind of initiation to belong to this group. Credentials are

everything. Belonging to this group is seen as an achievement.

## Treasure Honor

What ever you do, do not embarrass or compromise others in the group. Your word is your bond and you can be counted upon.

## Adhere to Tradition

New thought is not appreciated, we like doing things the old way. We value the historic and original as the proper way of doing things.

## Show Fortitude

Don't complain and don't take the easy way out. Work hard and suffer in silence. Those who "suffer" the most without complaining are prized.

## Be Fatalistic
Bad things happen, it's just how the world works don't be surprised and don't expect anything else.

## Be Ostentatious
Showing off your abilities, power and success is part of belonging. Status is achieved through visible means of success.

## Exert Prowess
Flaunt your skill and capability and make sure that everyone knows what you can do. Skill matters and must be shown and acknowledged.

## Shun Trading
You do not work for money you work for honor and loyalty. Money is not the main goal. To seek money is to dishonor the work.

## Dispense Largesse
You rise in status as you are more generous. The giving of gifts is a sign of your status and power.

## Make Rich Use of Leisure
Leisure should be devoted to the arts or to charity. You should be productive in some way that is not monetary and that gives you public visibility and status.

Think about how YOU live these values. Do you see them at work in your family? Where else might you see them? Remember the goal is protection and that these values form a system and are interdependent.

---

## *Effective Values*

This system is newer and focused on exchange. These values were found in the domain of merchants, traders and business. Now, however, they are found in all walks of life.

### Shun Force

Coercion and force are not to be used to get people's participation. You do not want to make enemies by using intimidation or violence.

### Come to Voluntary Agreement

People need to agree from their own free will. Agreements are negotiated and serve the needs and desires of all parties.

### Be Honest
Tell the truth and state how things really are. Don't engender false expectations of hide important facts and circumstances.

### Collaborate
Work with others to obtain your goals. Relationships are important as are partnerships of various kinds. Working together, each looks out for the other and shares learning and opportunities.

### Compete
Do your best to be better than others in your field. Grow yourself by doing each project better than the last one.

### Respect Contracts
Create agreements that are strong and serve all parties, then keep those contracts as you keep your word.

### Use Initiative & Enterprise
Be creative and think in new ways. Be the first to bring up a new idea or way of doing things. Create new opportunities and be the first to implement them.

## Be Open to Inventiveness & Novelty

Be open-minded and pay attention to new possibilities, where ever they may be found. Then make good use of them.

## Be Effective

Make sure that what you do achieves the ends you had in mind. Make sure that your actions meet the goals, needs and desires of those you are working with and for.

## Promote Comfort & Convenience

Establish yourself as one who can make life easier and more satisfying for others.

## Dissent for the Task

Openly state problems or issues you notice so that the result will be to everyone's satisfaction. Don't hide tribulations, troubles or problems.

## Invest for Productivity

Make sure you have the resources to increase your capacity, capability and to improve the quality of what you do.

## Be Industrious

Work hard and be tireless in the pursuit of your goals.

## Be Thrifty

Waste as little as possible and conserve whatever you can.

**Be Optimistic**
Do not become overcome by experiences or circumstances. Know always that a better, more productive time awaits.

Think about how YOU live these values. Do you see them at work in your family? Where else might you see them? Remember the goal is effectiveness and that these values form a system and are interdependent.

# Real Life Examples and Applications

When I work with clients I ask a series of questions that apply in two ways:
1. What do you experience every day?
2. What would you *like* to experience every day?

The answers to these questions tell me:
- What lives in the culture (yes families have culture)

- What the client prefers

- What others s/he lives with prefer

- The gap between the client and the family

- The preferred direction for change and how well it matches the families goals

- The cost and length of time it will take to make a change

- The likelihood that there are potential problems waiting to surface

The next two examples show the over all tendency in the family as seen by one member. The first one, in blue, indicates what that family member sees as alive in the family. In other words, what the family member believes s/he must adhere to and what is present in his/her everyday experience.

The second example, in red, shows what that family member prefers.

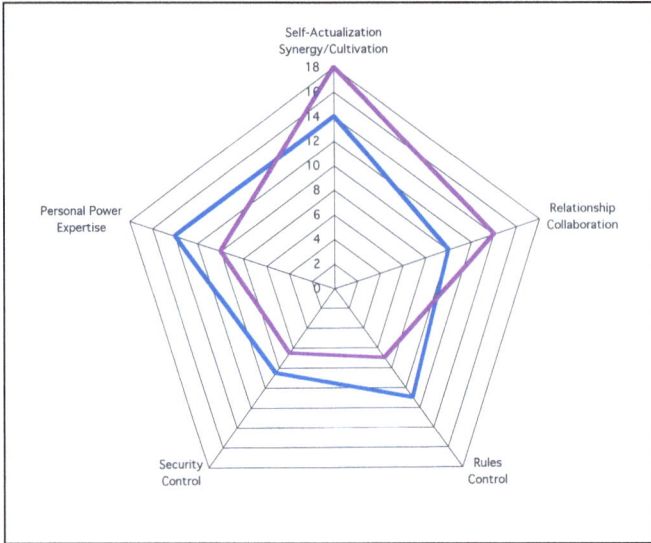

## **Figure 1 – Lived Values**

You can see that there is not an exact match. This means that at least *some* compromise has been made. Understanding that compromise and making it conscious can allow for a renewed and more satisfying relationship.

# Work Pages

## Defining your Values

### *Protective Values*

Which of these values do you see at play in your family? Jot down short examples of as many as you can.

_____

_____

_____

_____

_____

_____

_____

_____

_____

_____

_____

_____

_____

_____

_____

_____

_____

_____

_____

How are these values rewarded??

_____

_____

_____

_____

_____

_____

_____

_____

How do you feel about this?

_____

_____

_____

_____

_____

_____

_____

_____

Do these values serve the family as a whole?
What are the real results of acting on these
values?

_____

_____

_____

_____

_____

_____

_____

_____

_____

What would need to change to make the family
more effective?

_____

_____

_____

_____

_____

_____

_____

_____

## Stories

What are the most often told stories that support these values?

_____

_____

_____

_____

_____

_____

_____

_____

_____

_____

_____

_____

_____

_____

_____

_____

_____

_____

_____

What are these stories trying to accomplish?

_____

_____

_____

_____

_____

_____

_____

_____

_____

Are they useful to the family? If so in what way?
If not why not?

_____

_____

_____

_____

_____

_____

_____

_____

_____

_____

_____

_____

_____

_____

_____

_____

_____

_____

What other stories might be honestly told that
would have a different impact?

_____

_____

_____

_____

_____

_____

_____

_____

_____

_____

_____

_____

_____

## *Effective Values*

Which of these values do you see at play in your family? Jot down short examples of as many as you can.

_____

_____

_____

_____

_____

_____

_____

_____

_____

_____

_____

_____

_____

_____

_____

_____

_____

_____

_____

_____

_____

How are these values rewarded?

_____

_____

_____

_____

_____

_____

_____

_____

_____

_____

How do you feel about this?

_____

_____

_____

_____

_____

_____

_____

_____

_____

Do these values serve the family as a whole?
What are the real results of acting on these
values?

_____

_____

_____

_____

_____

_____

_____

_____

_____

What would need to change to make the family
more effective?

_____

_____

_____

_____

_____

_____

_____

_____

_____

## Stories

What are the most often told stories that support these values?

_____

_____

_____

_____

_____

_____

_____

_____

_____

_____

_____

_____

_____

_____

_____

_____

_____

_____

_____

_____

What are these stories trying to accomplish?

_____

_____

_____

_____

_____

_____

_____

_____

_____

Are they useful to the family? If so in what way?
If not why not?

_____

_____

_____

_____

_____

_____

_____

_____

_____

_____

_____

_____

_____

_____

_____

_____

_____

_____

_____

What other stories might be honestly told that would have a different impact?

_____

_____

_____

_____

_____

_____

_____

_____

_____

_____

_____

_____

## *Competition*

List here those experiences that seem to reflect a tendency to Competition.

_____

_____

_____

_____

_____

_____

_____

_____

_____

_____

_____

_____

_____

_____

_____

_____

_____

_____

In your estimation, what kind of behaviors does each family member express that supports a tendency to be competitive?

**Parents**

_____

_____

_____

_____

_____

_____

_____

_____

**Spouse**

_____

_____

_____

_____

_____

_____

_____

_____

## Siblings

_____

_____

_____

_____

_____

_____

_____

_____

## You

_____

_____

_____

_____

_____

_____

_____

_____

_____

## *Collaboration*

List here those experiences that seem to reflect a tendency to Collaborate.

_____

_____

_____

_____

_____

_____

_____

_____

_____

_____

_____

_____

_____

_____

_____

_____

_____

_____

_____

_____

In your estimation, what kind of behavior does each family member have that supports a tendency for collaboration?

## Parents

_____

_____

_____

_____

_____

_____

_____

_____

## Spouse

_____

_____

_____

_____

_____

_____

_____

_____

## Siblings

_____

_____

_____

_____

_____

_____

_____

_____

_____

## You

_____

_____

_____

_____

_____

_____

_____

_____

_____

_____

## *Innovation*

List here those experiences that seem to reflect a tendency for Innovation.

_____

_____

_____

_____

_____

_____

_____

_____

_____

_____

_____

_____

_____

_____

_____

_____

_____

_____

_____

_____

_____

In your estimation, what kind of behavior does each family member have that supports a tendency for innovation?

**Parents**

_____

_____

_____

_____

_____

_____

_____

_____

**Spouse**

_____

_____

_____

_____

_____

_____

_____

_____

## Siblings

_____

_____

_____

_____

_____

_____

_____

_____

_____

## You

_____

_____

_____

_____

_____

_____

_____

_____

_____

_____

## Summary

Over all, what kind of basic culture does your family have? (Competitive, Collaborative or Innovative)

_____

_____

_____

_____

What kind of behaviors are most common in your family?

_____

_____

_____

What kinds of changes would improve your family relationships?

_____

_____

_____

_____

_____

What kinds of changes can *you* make in your own behavior to help bring these changes about?

_____

_____

_____

_____

_____

_____

_____

_____

_____

What actions can *you* take to help bring these changes about?

_____

_____

_____

_____

_____

_____

_____

_____

# Personal Notes

# Go Deeper

## *A Bonus for You!*

Contact me for a FREE 30 minute Q&A on your workbook process.

Kathryn Alexander, MA is a coach devoted to helping people create a lasting legacy that is both ethically robust, personally and financially rewarding.

We provide:
- o Values Clarification.
- o Assessments for values, and relationship effectiveness.
- o Ethical coaching for both short and long-term issues.
- o Health and spiritual coaching

We can be reached at:
9116 E. Sprague Suite 585
Spokane, WA 99206
(303) 818-4147 or (866) 872-8623
kathryn@kathrynalexanderlive.com
www.kathrynalexanderlive.com

www.ingramcontent.com/pod-product-compliance
Lightning Source LLC
Chambersburg PA
CBHW041218270326
41931CB00001B/30